PRINCETON PAMPHLETS—No. 6

JOHANN GEORG HAMANN

AN EXISTENTIALIST

by
Walter Lowrie

WIPF & STOCK · Eugene, Oregon

Wipf and Stock Publishers
199 W 8th Ave, Suite 3
Eugene, OR 97401

Johann Georg Hamann
An Existentialist
By Lowrie, Walter
ISBN 13: 978-1-4982-8313-7
Publication date 2/22/2016
Previously published by Princeton Theological Seminary, 1950

JOHANN GEORG HAMANN
An Existentialist

I.
THE MAN AND HIS LIFE

No work of Hamann has been translated into English, and, so far as I know, almost nothing has been written about him, except a contemptuous column in the *Encyclopaedia Britannica*—where also Kierkegaard is coldly dismissed in a paragraph of half that length. But a great deal has been written in Germany; and Princetonians may be interested to know that all of his works and most of the books which have been written about him are to be found in the libraries of the University and the Theological Seminary.[1]

[1] The first edition of H.'s collected works was made thirty-three years after his death by Friedrich Roth: *Hamann's Schriften*, 7 vols., Berlin, 1821-25. An 8th volume prepared by Wiener was added in 1842. Roth lived in Munich, where he had the help of Jacobi in preparing this great edition; and yet Jacobi's voluminous correspondence with H. could not be included because the publisher of Jacobi's works would not allow this part to be republished. But H.'s works stand in need of interpretation, and this is furnished for the more important works by Gildemeister: *Johann Georg Hamann, des Magus in Norden, Leben und Schriften*, Gotha, 1863-75, in 3 vols., to which 2 vols., which contain the correspondence with Jacobi, were added ten years later. I am more deeply indebted to Moritz Petri: *Johann Georg Hamann, Schriften und Briefen*, 4 vols., Hanover, 1872-74. These books provide apparatus enough for the student, but I add the names of more recent works. A comparison between Hamann and Kierkegaard was made by Rodemann in a doctoral dissertation, *Hamann und Kierkegaard*, presented at Erlangen in 1912 and published at Gütersloh in 1922. A more important work is by E. Weber: *Zwei Propheten des Irrationalismus, J. G. Hamann und S. Kierkegaard*, published in numbers 1 and 2 of *Neue kirchliche Zeitung* for 1927 (XXXVIII Jahrgang, pp. 23-55, 77-125). This work was used by Torsten Bohlin, *Kierkegaards dogmatische Anschauung* (German translation 1929, pp. 55ff.). I would mention also Fritz Blanke, *J. G. Hamann als Theologe*, 1928, No. 130 of *Gemeinvorständliche Vorträge*. More recently a Danish pastor, Tage Schack, had half completed a work on Hamann when he was put to death by the Germans for his boldness in pronouncing a eulogy at the funeral of a Dane who had been executed for complicity in underground resistance. This incomplete work was published in 1948 in Copenhagen with the title *Johan Georg Hamann*, Tidehvervs Forlag. From Niels Thulstrup, Secretary of the Kierkegaard Society in Denmark, I learn that there has just been published in Salzburg, through the Otto Müller Verlag, a *Hamann Biografie* of 518 pages by Professor Joseph Nadler. This book has not yet reached me, but I am comforted to know that I am not the only man in my generation who admires Hamann.

My attention has been tardily called to a couple of references to H. in American publications. In 1901 J. A. Walz had something to say about H.'s "attitude towards America," in an article on "The American Revolution in German Literature," which was published in Vol. XVI of *Modern Language Notes*. And recently Philip Merlan contributed two "notes" which he calls *Parva Hamanniana* to the *Journal of the History of Ideas*, Vol. IX (June 1948) and Vol. X (October 1949)—the first note being an unfortunate attempt to depict H. as a "spokesman for the middle class," because of the enthusiasm he expressed for the mercantile profession in

In Germany H. fought almost single-handed against the Illuminism of the eighteenth century, and hence it was not till the following century his works could be commonly read with a sympathetic understanding. Among the men of the nineteenth century who were profoundly influenced by him was Kierkegaard. In this author, who lived a hundred years before his day, Kierkegaard recognized his *alter ego*, and he discovered him just at the time when he most needed the help H. could give. It was in his student days when he had registered in his *Journal* the conviction that Christianity could not endure the searching light of philosophy. He hailed him at once as "Emperor!", and he remarked that everything he wrote bore his own image and superscription. In my *Kierkegaard* I registered the opinion—which has perhaps more truth than evidence on its side— that no other author influenced him so profoundly. It would be interesting to trace this influence in detail by comparing the writings of these two men. Here, of course, I should be going too far afield, if I were to follow this enticing lead. Rodemann and Weber have made such a study in the works mentioned in the footnote.

In one of the early volumes of his *Journal* Kierkegaard noted the impression made upon him when he saw that H., after reading one of Hume's sharpest objections to Christianity, was not in the least disturbed in his faith but remarked quietly, "Yes, that's exactly how it is." At first he was offended by a remark which H. repeated several times: "I would rather hear wisdom from Baalam's ass or from a philosopher against his will than from an angel or an apostle." He thought this saying almost blasphemous, but in the end he made it his own. And evidently it was appropriate to Hume. H. had been reading the chapter on miracles in Hume's famous *Inquiry Concerning the Human Understanding*, in which the skeptical philosopher says: "So that upon the whole we may conclude, not only that the Christian religion was at first attended with miracles, but even to this day cannot be believed by any reasonable person without one. Mere reason is not sufficient to convince us of its veracity; and whoever is moved by faith to assent to it, is conscious of a continued miracle in his own person, which subverts all the principles of his

---

the first book he published and almost at once repudiated; the second treating of his casual acquaintance with the interesting but notorious Schmohl. It will be seen that this is indeed a very "slight" contribution to a knowledge of H., as the title modestly admits. But I too must admit that the title, *Parva Hamanniana*, would be appropriate to what I am writing here.

Someone may be grateful to me for setting down here all of Kierkegaard's references to H. *Either/Or* I, 201. *Fear and Trembling*, motto after the title page. *Repetition*, 34f. *Stages*, 138 ("wise man"), 100, 104, 122 (Bah!), 187 (*periissem*). *Concept of Dread*, 85 ("greatest humorist," cf. II A 75), 145n. *Fragments*, 42f. *Postscript*, 223f., 258n., 495. My *Kierkegaard*, 164ff., 256. My *Short Life*, 108f., 115f. I add references to the *Journal*, though only in my two biographies have some of them been translated. *Papirer* I A 100, 233, 234, 237; II A 2, 12 (p. 15), 75, 105, 114, 730; IV A 122; VIII A 151; IX A 45.

· 4 ·

understanding, and gives him a determination to believe what is most contrary to custom and experience." Kierkegaard was struck by H.'s comment: "Hume may have said this with a scornful and critical air, yet all the same, this is orthodoxy and a witness to the truth from the mouth of an enemy and persecutor—all his doubts are proofs of his proposition." His conclusive retort to Hume was appreciatively copied by Kierkegaard in his *Journal*: "*Incredibile sed verum.* Lies and fictitious romances must be plausible, and so too hypotheses and fables; but not the truths and basic propositions of our faith." But H. had a great admiration for this Scottish skeptic, in spite of his skepticism, and he meant no disparagement of his friend Kant when he described him as "the Prussian Hume." He had taken pains to translate Hume's *Dialogues on Natural religion,* and, though he refrained from publishing it, he showed the manuscript to Kant, who, in the opinion of Professor Kemp Smith, was led by this to adopt a negative attitude towards natural religion.

Because of his influence upon Kierkegaard I was prompted to delve into the works of H., and my curiosity was sharpened by Kierkegaard's description of him as "the most humorous author in Christendom." I had no difficulty in discovering good reason for this superlative appreciation; for in no other author is the trait of humor so pervasive, even in his most serious passages. Mark Twain was, of course, a great humorist, but he did not permit his humor to intrude when he was dealing with so serious a subject as Joan of Arc. But H. in reviewing one of the latest works of Voltaire (and it need hardly be said that the Enlightenment took Voltaire very seriously) permitted himself to say of the old man's style that "its fire is not quenched, and its worm dieth not." I found, however, that it was a much more difficult matter to discover his *meaning.* I was prepared to delve, but had not expected to find the digging so hard. I hardly would have had the courage to persevere, if before long my diligence and the sweat of my brow had not been rewarded by the discovery of a few nuggets of gold which convinced me that this mine was well worth working. I accomplished almost nothing when I tried to work it alone, but I was greatly aided by such astute interpreters as Gildemeister and Petri.

It is not easy to account for the obscurity of H.'s style when he was writing for publication; for his letters were written lucidly, and even in his works he shows an extraordinary talent for coining striking and felicitous phrases. A German author has collected such gems, and they fill a large volume. H. sometimes deplored the obscurity of his style, for he was unhappy over the failure to make himself understood by his contemporaries, but he made no serious effort to overcome this defect. It may be remarked that the next generation understood him better, because the publication of his letters threw a flood of light upon the darkest passages of his works. He was hampered in speech by the thickness of his tongue, and there seems to have been a similar impediment in his mind which hindered him from writing clearly when he was writing for publication. He said expressively that he wielded his pen like an axe to hew his way through a dense forest. He spoke of himself as "a wooden man," and was content if only his "wooden arm," like a signpost on the highway, pointed wayfarers in the right direction. He knew that the style is the man, and that the leopard cannot change its spots. In fact, everything he wrote—and not least of all the significant title pages on which he disguised himself by a pseudonym—bears unmistakably his personal signature. In a letter to Kant he defended his peculiar style on the ground that it corresponded to his peculiar nature, noting that every animal has its own gait corresponding to its structure. "One goes by leaps and bounds, like a grasshopper; another moves in a continuous course, like a blind-worm, which because of its structure needs to keep in a rut. One goes in a straight line, another in a curve, and the crab walks sideways. According to Hogarth's theory, the snake-line is the essential element in pictorial art." In the same letter he boasts: "In my mimic style there is a stricter logic and a more firmly cemented cohesion than in the conceptions of lively pates whose ideas, as Pope says, are like the shimmering colors of watered silk." By his "mimic style" he meant that instead of using words as counters he sought in every way to evoke realities.

About the humor which bubbles up even in the most serious passages, he says to Kant, "May I not be allowed to sport with my wit, as Isaac did with his wife Rebecca—if only I take care not to pass beneath the windows of the lustful Philistines?" (referring to the story recounted in Gen. 28, which is not often mentioned today but was seldom ignored by the early illustrators of the Bible). It seems that Kant was not convinced by H.'s arguments, for when at a later date he had reason to ask his opinion on a certain subject he begged him "to write in human language," confessing that he did not possess the gift of the interpretation of tongues. It is a consolation to learn that even Kant, who was an intimate friend, had difficulty in understanding H., and still more to hear that Goethe, who certainly knew German better than I, had to read one of his works three times before he got a notion what it was about. H. himself was forced to admit that after a long lapse of time, when he no longer could recall the mood which prompted him to write, he could not make sure what he had meant to say.

The most essential reason for the obscurity of H.'s style is that it was discontinuous, like "the gait of a grasshopper," revealing thereby a characteristic of his spiritual structure which caused him to abhor theoretical systems and to shun therefore even "the straightforward mathematical form" in which they are presented by the use of mere words or algebraic signs. This he called "the tyranny of Apollo." He would go back behind the words to the things themselves. He was therefore distrustful of the technical language of philosophy, and he repudiated "the world-wisdom which out of a universal knowledge of possibilities constructs a universal ignorance of the actual." Although realities are doubtless basically related, they appear to us as separate things, like islands which rise from the floor of the sea, without any connection by bridge or ferry, and therefore, like Socrates, H. expected his readers "to be able to swim" and denied them even the help of illative propositions.[2]

Another cause of H.'s obscurity is what he called "a holy frugality in the use of words." At the thought that he might be using a word needlessly he blushed like a maiden whose purity is called in question. Hence all his works are exceedingly short. If they had been longer, it would not take so long to read them. Jean Paul, though he had no close spiritual kinship with H., refers to him often with admiration, and it was not meant as a hostile criticism of his style when he said, "The great Hamann is a profound heaven full of telescopic stars—and many flecks of cloud which no eye can dissolve. Brevity is clarity—except in the case of Hamann, whose commas contain at times planetary systems, whose periods are galaxies of suns and whose words are sometimes sentences."

The obscurity of his style is due also to the fact that he barely alludes to matters which he assumes, too flatteringly, that his readers must know. In the first place, his writings are saturated with the language of Luther's Bible, which not even Germans can be expected to know thoroughly. In the second place he supposes that the merest hint is enough to recall the stories of Greek and Roman mythology which once were familiar to all cultivated persons. This is exasperating in our day when we have to confess that allusions no longer allude. Also, alas, he very frequently quotes ancient classical authors, without translating the "dead languages" in which they wrote. After seventeen hundred years of Christian history H. had not the same reason that Jerome and Augustine had to repress his love for these pagan authors, and he felt free to value them for their wit, if not for

---

[2] Kierkegaard in a passage of the *Postscript* (p. 224, which I translate here afresh) recognized that a "desultory" style, the gait of the grasshopper, was appropriate to one who like H. was averse to writing "connectedly": "I would not conceal my admiration for Hamann, though I am ready to admit that the elasticity of his thought lacks balance and his supernatural buoyancy lacks self-control —if he were to have worked connectedly. But in his brief sayings there is the originality of genius and a pregnancy of form which is in perfect keeping with his desultory way of slinging out a thought. With his whole life and soul, even to the last drop of his blood, he is concentrated upon one word, the passionate protest of a highly gifted genius against a system of actual being." In an early entry in his *Journal* (I A 234) he says: "At a time when it is a matter of course for one author to pillage from another, it is a pleasure to encounter men whose individuality so stamps and mints every word with their own effigy that it must compel every one who meets with such a word in a strange place to say to the writer in question, 'Render unto Caesar the things that are Caesar's.'"

their wisdom. The lack of understanding on the part of his readers H. was disposed to attribute to "an ignorance in the will"; but his unkinder critics were not willing to admit this, and one of them praised his writings maliciously by exclaiming:

> Wahrhaftig, das ist schön!
> Der teufel selbst kann's nicht verstehen!

I have been told that I ought to give "a synoptic characterization of Hamann's conception of Christianity." I cannot plead that there is not room enough here for the brief statement which is required of me; and I cannot say that this task is impossible—but only that I am unequal to it. The shorter such a statement is, the harder it must be. The reader will find here sufficient material for his own characterization; and I venture to summarize it only by explaining what I mean by calling H. an "existentialist." In the title of this paper I have used this word to recommend H. to a generation which has forgotten him but professes to be interested in "existentialism"—without quite knowing what this word means. It may seem far-fetched to call H. an existentialist, seeing that he seldom used the word *Existenz* and never attributed to it a special significance. But for this very reason we can the more clearly discern here what this *thing* means about which people talk so much and describe by a word which is not sufficiently descriptive.[3]

[3] One who essays to determine the character of Kierkegaard's "existentialism," relying upon the English translation, will be confounded by the fact that the word "existence" is used not only for *Existens*, but also and more frequently for *Tilvaerelse*, which is equivalent to the German *Dasein* and is used without any special significance. Recent as the English translation of Kierkegaard is, it antedates the pother about "existentialism," and therefore the translators could not have foreseen the necessity of distinguishing between *Existens* and *Tilvaerelse*. The latter word is translated by "existential" even in so important a passage as that on page 99 of the *Postscript*, which ought to read: "Such a thing as a logical system is possible, but a system of actual being is not possible." It is to be hoped that before long the reprinting of Kierkegaard's works will make it possible to introduce this distinction and to make a few other changes in nomenclature. Professor Swenson, when he was collaborating with me to insure uniformity in the translation of Kierkegaard, said disconsolately that it might take several generations to fix the nomenclature, as it did in the case of the translation of Kant. But I can think now of only four important terms which ought to be altered—and among them is *not* the word "dread" as the translation of *Angst*. As things are now, the school-boy essays and the doctoral dissertations which profess to deal with Kierkegaard's existentialism in reliance upon the English translation can hardly be more than a battle about words—for which neither Kierkegaard nor H. are in any way responsible, since both of them were intent upon getting behind words and logomachies so as to deal with realities. Both of them in their several generations were staunch antagonists of the idolatrous worshipers of Reason who soar above the realities of life and weave logical systems, cobwebs of the brain, ethereal substitutes for our primary intuitions of the facts of human existence, whether sensible or spiritual (including the fact that we exist, "the noble *sum*," as H. said, "which must not be made subordinate to *cogito*"). They both fought the good fight against Idealism in its Protean forms. Heidegger, Jaspers, Sartre and *compagna*

· 8 ·

H. was an existentialist first of all in his relation to God—the living God, not an idea—who of old actually performed great acts in favor of his people, and still continues to perform them through a providence which numbers even the hairs of our head. Hence history as a whole—and not only sacred history—is God's speech to men who have ears to hear. The incarnation of God in Christ, though it is incredible, is nevertheless true, because it is necessary. It is not an idea but a fact, and it is in keeping with God's many acts of condescension to man. As an existentialist H. laid emphasis upon the bodily man, the man of flesh and blood (or of *carne y hueso*, as Unamuno prefers to say); therefore man's response to God must be a response of the whole man, of his passions as well his intellect—faith is love and practical obedience. This is his Christian "existentialism" (if I may use the word); and in what follows enough will be found to implement this summary statement.[4]

The man Hamann must be known, if one would understand his writings; for he thought as a whole man, not only with his head but with his viscera. Therefore something must be said here, however briefly, about this singular man and his strange life.

Johann Georg Hamann was born in Königsberg on August 27, 1730. His father, the principal surgeon of that city, was highly respected for his character, rather than for his profession, which in those days of bleeding, cupping, the application of leeches, and the prescription of baths was hardly superior to that of the barber. Because of the esteem in which this surgeon was held, the public bathing establishment of the city was put under his charge, and this good doctor prized no title more highly than that which was bestowed upon him by the people, who called him the Old-Town Bather. This

---

bella have this in common with them; but by calling themselves existentialists they betray the fact that they are really on the side of the enemy with its theories and "isms." It is significant that Kierkegaard never used the word "existentialism" but spoke only of "existence" and of "the exister" and of "existential." Someone who is abler than I ought to silence all this talk about Kierkegaard's "existentialism" by giving a lucid and sober account of the sheerly untheoretical meaning Kierkegaard attached to existence. Sufficient data are to be found in one volume, the *Postscript*. Out of this bag one might pluck a smooth round stone to smite the Philistine and rout the whole host of the enemy.

[4] H. is an existentialist in his conception of language as the expression of truth. For truth is not something abstract but a reflection of reality—reality which is independent of us but encompasses us on all sides, and which indeed we *are*. For the apprehension of truth man is dependent upon words, and the discovery of the right word is a creative act, not unlike the creative word of God. But words reproduce reality only in signs and symbols. Naked truth is not for us: we need to have it clothed in words, which hide it as well as reveal it. "Truth," said H., "will not permit highwaymen to approach her too closely. She clothes herself with so many garments that one might be doubtful of discovering her body. How terrified the highwaymen would be were they to get their will and see before them the dreadful spectre—Truth!"

gave H. occasion to say that he revered his father's bath-tub just as Socrates did the stool of his mother the midwife. The surgeon and his wife, who came of a good bourgeois family in Lubeck, spared no pains in educating their two sons, and Johann when he was sixteen years old entered the University of Königsberg. He entered it as a student of theology, but abandoned this study on the ground that his tongue was too thick for public speaking. Rather inconsequentially he turned to the study of law, but did not follow it long; for he conceived a contempt for bread and butter studies and devoted himself to languages and philosophy. He spent five years in the university and accumulated a great deal of curious learning but did not try for the master's degree. In those days there was no such thing as a doctorate in philosophy, and even so great a man as Kant was not called Doctor but Magister. Young H. learned Hebrew in order to read the Old Testament and Arabic in order to read the Koran; in Greek and Latin he had of course been thoroughly trained before he entered the university; he knew French and English well, and before long he learned to read Spanish and Italian. His subsequent writings attest the diligence with which he studied philology and philosophy.

On leaving the university in 1752 he was eager to see something of the world and grasped the opportunity of going to Courland, where for four years he served as tutor in the families of two different noblemen who had estates not far from Riga, where the Rector of the Gymnasium was Johann Gottlieb Lindner, who had been his friend from childhood and his companion in the university. With this friend he maintained a frequent and intimate correspondence as long as he lived. In Riga he was on a footing of intimacy with a family of successful merchants named Berens who came there from Rostock. One of the sons, Johann Christoph Berens, had been his schoolmate in Königsberg and for a long time was his most intimate friend. This man had studied at Göttingen, had travelled widely and had completely absorbed the prevailing culture of his time. As a man of the world he was diligent in business, serviceable to his country, and a fervent champion of the Enlightenment. By him H. was completely won over to the central tenet of the Enlightenment, the fond belief that "the best world" would result surely and soon from the progress of commerce and industry. We may reflect now that this chiliastic superstition was pretty much on a line with Marxism.

In 1755, at his friend's suggestion, H. translated a French work by Bougeuil on political economy and commerce, adding a chapter of his own which breathes the utopian enthusiasm of the French Encyclopedia. In that mood he gladly accepted the suggestion of the Berens brothers that he go to England as their representative. In suggesting this, Christoph Berens was prompted not only by his interest in the greatest good of the greatest number, but by a personal affection for his friend and the hope that a man of such evident genius as a writer might become a prosperous merchant. The journey to London gave H. an opportunity to see the world. He set out from Riga in July 1756, stopped with his parents until October, then went on to Berlin, stayed a while in Lubeck with his mother's family, and after passing through Bremen and Holland reached London on April 18, 1757.

We do not know precisely what happened in London to discourage the young man. It may have been only the painful recognition of the fact that he completely lacked the talents required of a merchant. He fell into bad company, which led him into riotous living, by which he was soon reduced to poverty and moral misery. He wrote to no one during all the time he spent in England, and neither his parents nor the Berens were informed of his address. But his extremity was God's opportunity, and in London he experienced a thorough conversion through the reading of the Bible. When he had read the Old Testament once and the New Testament twice without experiencing any edification, he reflected that he ought to read the Bible through again "with greater attention, in a more orderly way, with a sharper hunger, regarding everything written therein as addressed expressly to me." As a consequence of this disciplined reading, during which he made copious notes, the light shone upon him, and he was saved. This experience made him a biblicist, but it did not make him a literalist; for without a very free interpretation, like that of the author of the Epistle to the Hebrews, he could not apply every word to himself and recognize like St. Paul that "these things were written for our learning." "The Holy Spirit," he affirmed, "is the only safe interpreter of the Scriptures which he wrote"; but above all human interpretations he preferred the *Gnomon* of Bengel.

Of the notes on the Bible which he made in London only about a fifth have been published; but the Confession which he wrote at the same time was published in full, as it deserved to be, although it was written for his father and his brother and perhaps a few friends. It is a frank and genuine confession, which is marred only by the recurrence of Pietistic phrases, with which he was familiar in his youth, but which he never used again. Having come to himself like the Prodigal Son, he learned to know himself more profoundly than Apollo thought of requiring of men in the motto which everyone read on entering his temple at Delphi. He discovered that self-knowledge is a descent into hell—he spoke frequently of *die Höllenfahrt der Selbsterkenntnis*—in which he beheld not only human depravity but the impotence of human wisdom. He was convinced that every man, even if he be a genius or a hero, must at times be prompted to exclaim like the crowned psalmist of Israel, "I am a worm and no man." He learned that the worst sins are not of the body but of the spirit. "The body is the garment of the soul: it covers its nakedness and shame. Sensual and ambitious men ascribe their shameful tendencies to their blood and to the fibres of their body. But how repulsive man might be, if the body did not set bounds to him!" "The last fruit of all world-wisdom is the recognition of human ignorance and weakness. This cornerstone is also the millstone which grinds to powder all men's sophistries. So our reason is just what St. Paul calls the law—and the law of reason is holy, just and good. But is it given to make us wiser? No more than the law was given the Jews to make them righteous, but rather to convince us of the opposite, namely, how unreasonable our reason is, and that our errors must increase because of it, as sin increased because of the law." "Our own existence and the existence of things outside us must be *believed* and can be ascertained in no other way. Therefore what is believed does not need to be proved, and a proposition may be proved incontrovertibly without for this reason being believed. Faith is not the work of reason. By an attack from this side, therefore, it cannot be overcome, since faith is no more due to reasons than is taste or sight."

This he learned from David Hume! In this connection H. remarks that there are proofs of the truth which in themselves are as far from being edifying as the application to which they are put. He refers to the report of Lactantius that a professor of philosophy adduced such convincing proofs of the immortality of the soul that his hearers went out and committed suicide. H. learned from the Bible (as did Soloviev) that the Incarnation does not stand alone, precariously, as a solitary instance of God's humility, but that the act of creation itself, God's poetic authorship, was a humiliation on God's part (not self-glorification, as some think), and that God humbled himself again in becoming the author of the Scriptures. "What a humiliation it is for God to reveal himself in human language! The Holy Spirit became a writer of history, recounting the lowliest and most despicable events, yea, foolish and sinful acts, in order to speak to us in our language about our situation."[5]

It should be recognized that H. experienced a conversion which was not only religious but intellectual, a conversion away from the worship of Reason and back to a hearty appreciation of the *realities* of Biblical revelation. The concreteness of Biblical thought is existential in the fullest sense of the word. *Die Wirklichkeit der Hebraeer* is the striking title of a book by Oskar Goldberg. But the sense of reality this author discovers in the Bible is hardly characteristic of the Hebrews as a race. Kierkegaard remarked that the success of the Jews in dealing with money is due to the fact that money is

[5] In London he wrote also reflections of a general character, which he called *Brocken*. He explained the use of this title by a reference to John 6:12. Since Kierkegaard doubtless saw this work, it is likely that by it he was prompted to call his philosophical reflections *Smuler*, which is the word the Danish Bible uses in the same passage. This seems to justify Professor Swenson in calling this book *Fragments*—and confounds me for opposing his choice.

the most abstract thing. One is compelled to think of Spinoza, the unhappy Spanish Jew of Amsterdam, who in his lonely garret formulated an idea of God which is so perfectly abstract that it is equivalent to atheism. Moses Mendelssohn felt aggrieved when H. spoke of him as an atheist, whereas he too had been at pains to prove the existence of God—as an idea. It was in this connection H. said that "to deny the existence of God or to prove it amounts to precisely the same thing." Mendelssohn himself had said in reply to Lavater's effort to convert him to Christianity, that he could perceive no difference between the idea of God held by liberal Jews and that of Christian Rationalists like Lessing. In fact, both were nothing but *ideas*. After all, how could Nathan the Wise, were he to adopt the name of a Christian, be better off than he was as Lessing describes him?

But the Bible deals with realities. God and the great acts which he performed for the deliverance of his people were not merely instructive ideas: the people actually were saved by passing through the Red Sea, they were healed by looking at the brazen serpent, by the manna they were actually fed *ex opere operato*, and by the water from the rock their thirst was actually quenched. It should not be forgotten that the New Testament is a part of the Bible and shares the character of *Wirklichkeit* which is evident in the Hebrew Scriptures. And inasmuch as the sacraments of the New Covenant were understood in the light of God's great works of old, it cannot reasonably be thought that they are less real—that "the laver of regeneration" does not really regenerate, and that one who breaks the bread in remembrance of Christ Jesus does not really receive the true manna which cometh down out of heaven. But many besides Mrs. Mary Baker G. Eddy use a key to the Scriptures which has been fabricated by idealistic philosophy. This needs to be said to make clear how it was that by his absorption in the thought of the Bible H. became an uncompromising opponent of the Enlightenment, which transformed realities into ideas, and a "metacritic" (to use the word he coined) of the critical philosophy of Kant, questioning "the purism of *pure* reason" and the naïve assumption of "the good will."

It is not clear how H., in spite of his poverty, managed to get home soon after his conversion. But we know that he left London in June 1758, that after a brief visit to his father, who was then a widower, he reached Riga not later than August and remained there till March of the following year.

In Riga he was heartily received by his friends. In spite of the singularity of his character, he had a talent for making friends and keeping them. Even the Berens family did not reproach him for his failure as a merchant. But Christoph Berens, who at that time was absent on a mission to the Court of Russia, was deeply chagrined to learn that his bosom friend had become, as he understood it, a bigoted Christian. Though he had to renounce the hope of making him a merchant, he was intent upon reconverting him to the rationalism of the Enlightenment in order that as an author he might attain the fame which his genius seemed to promise. He was annoyed by the stubborn resistance his letters encountered, and it is likely that his annoyance prompted him to oppose the proposal of marriage H. had made to his sister Katharine. This attitude of Christoph put an end to his stay in Riga, and he returned to the home of his father, who was crippled by paralysis and stood in need of his assistance.

Christoph Berens pursued him with his letters, and receiving no reply to them (in fact they were never opened), he recruited J. G. Lindner, H.'s regular correspondent, as a "neutral" mediator. Lindner too compliantly accepted this dangerous role. His letter has not been preserved, but from the reply, which was a torrent of sarcasm, we can well understand that Lindner promptly retired from the perilous position in which he had been put—but without interrupting his affectionate correspondence with H. This story must be told because it was part of the provocation which prompted H. to write what he accounted "the beginning of his authorship," *Socratic Memorabilia*, which will be considered later.

The four years H. spent in his father's house before the old surgeon died were the happiest of his whole life and the most productive. The duty of assisting his father was so obvious that no notion of taking a more public part in life could occur to him. Yet this duty left him at leisure to do what he liked best: to read and to write. It is amazing how much erudition he acquired during this period of leisure, and it is amazing that he was able to digest it. His letters show how eagerly he devoured all the contemporary literature of Europe, in French and in English as well as in German; and when he was struck by what seemed to him a literary event, he wrote about it in a militant spirit. He was able to appraise this modern literature against the background of the classics, both Christian and pagan. Daily and in large doses he read, marked, learned and inwardly digested the Old Testament in Hebrew and the New Testament in Greek, though he commonly quoted them in Luther's translation. He also regarded it as a duty to devote definite periods of time to reading the Greek poets, historians and philosophers. With the Latin poets he had been familiar from his youth.

We may wonder that this sturdy champion of Biblical Christianity had so hearty an appreciation of pagan wit and wisdom. In fact he had adopted as his motto the proud boast of the comic poet,

Homo sum, nihil humani a me alienum puto,

and this he thought was expressed in St. Paul's proud words, "All things are yours." Therefore he could say, "To me every book is a

Bible, and every occupation a prayer." This attitude characterized not only his reading but his choice of acquaintances; for not only Christians who sympathized with his position did he see frequently and correspond with regularly, but also liberal Christians, free-thinkers, Jews, and, in his last years, Roman Catholics. Though he loved these "enemies," he did not hesitate to attack them openly; and by this, strangely enough, he did not lose their friendship. Indeed, he made a fast friend of a stranger, von Moser, by attacking a book he had written. It was von Moser who first hailed him as "the Magus of the North," and to this new friend, whom he had often to thank for a hamper of game which was welcome to him and his hungry children, he applied the affectionate title, "lay brother."

After the death of his father H. was plagued almost to the end of his days by poverty and care. For the patrimony he received scarcely availed to pay his debts, and with astonishing indiscretion he had acquired responsibility for "a housewife and four wholesome children," which were at once his joy and his burden. A wholesome peasant girl, unable to read or write, who was the only servant in the house and his father's faithful nurse, attracted H. so powerfully that, strive as he would against the temptation, he had four children by her without a legal marriage. What we would describe as a civil marriage he called *Gewissensehe*, implying, I suppose, the resolution to keep himself only unto her so long as they both should live. He made no secret of this relationship, but though he called it a marriage, he never spoke of the mother of his children as his wife.

This is an obscure story upon which H. did not deign to cast much light. Yet this brief reference to it cannot be omitted, since it accounts for the perplexity of the last twenty-five years of his life. Strangest of all is the fact that a man so profoundly religious did not have this union legitimatized by the State and blessed by the Church. He said in one place that it was better for the mother and the children that things should be left as they were. But this explanation is enigmatical. To us it is astonishing that for this unconventional union H. was not reproached by his many clerical friends. At first his "confessor" charged him with seducing an innocent girl, but it seems that his old father defended him, and in the end this pious family, besides holding daily prayers at home, went together to Church and together received the Holy Communion. Except for Herder, who named his first son after H., none of his friends were invited to stand as godparents to his children. The mother and father, because of the singularity of their relationship, assumed the duties of sponsors.

H. was diligent in instructing his son—so diligent that at ten years of age little Hans had read the New Testament in Greek three times and was about to start the study of Hebrew. But for his daughters he could do little, and his wife could do nothing—not even so much as teach them to sew. It is cheering to remark at this point that H.'s faith in divine providence was justified by the fact that all his children grew up to be persons of some distinction, his son becoming a teacher in the gymnasium of Königsberg. But there was another cloud which had no silver lining. His brother, only two years younger than he, whom he loved devotedly, and for whom he found a place as teacher in the gymnasium at Riga, was never a satisfaction to anybody, and from indolence he finally sunk into such complete imbecility that he never left his bed and lived only to eat and sleep. H. was appointed his legal guardian and until his death spared a room for him in a house which was not large enough for the children. After the brother's death H. proposed to write "The Idiot's Apology," but got no farther than this engaging title. We can well imagine that the presence of an idiot brother added to the squalid conditions in which H. was condemned to live. Weather permitting, a guest might be invited into the garden, which he described as "an ill-kept vegetable garden, a summer house, and the Grove of Mamre with a view of the fields beyond the moat"; but illustrious friends could hardly be invited into the house, where the general living room was the kitchen over which the house-mother presided, and where the library had to serve as a bedroom for the father and his son. H. described all these hardships in his letters to intimate friends, yet he spoke of himself as a flourishing palm. His exuberant genius could not be quenched, but his literary productivity was hampered.

His literary productivity was hampered by the necessity of making a living for himself and his family. Although his learning fitted him for the post of a teacher, he recognized that the peculiarities of his disposition unfitted him for such a position. Von Moser found a place for him as tutor to a princeling in the south of Germany, but his unequal marriage unfitted him for that. Finally he found a job as French translator in the office of the collector of customs in Königsberg, where he was later advanced to the position of warden of the magazine, which included the use of a free dwelling, about which he had conflict with the widow of his predecessor. His salary of 40 *Thaler* a month, which even in those times was insufficient to support his family, had been reduced to 35 by the penuriousness of Frederick the Great (an injustice against which H. frequently complained in his books), and the extraordinary emoluments he was justified in expecting were absorbed by the Frenchmen whom the King had put in charge of the collection of taxes. Subservience to these thieving foreigners made his job distasteful to him, and it was unfortunate that as warden of the magazine he had little to do but waste his time by staying in the office.

H. kept a careful account of all income and expenditures, but scrupulous bookkeeping did not avail to keep the balance from coming out in the red. It may be supposed that from time to time his friends found ways of wiping out the deficits. At one moment, when he was preparing to make the tragic sacrifice of selling his library, Herder intervened to save it by sending him a considerable gift which he adroitly represented as a mortgage on his books. But his case seemed hopeless. H. accused himself of an inordinate appetite for food, especially for meat. His hunger for books, however, was still more ruinous. I note that on one occasion he paid for books ordered from London more than he received in a month for "sitting like Zacchaeus or Matthew at the receipt of custom." Though by his admirers he was hailed as the Magus of the North, which put him on a par with the Three Kings of the Orient, he preferred, on account of the rude conditions in which he lived, to call himself *Le Sauvage du Nord.*

Yet in spite of his poverty, in spite also of the contumely to which he was exposed for being an opponent of the liberal spirit of his time, he lived on intimate terms with his neighbor Immanuel Kant and with other lights of the University, including Professor Kraus (whom he called Crispus) and J. G. Lindner, who came later to Königsberg as professor, with Hippel, who for a long time was Mayor of Königsberg, with Herder, whom he regarded as his disciple, with Lavater, Claudius and Jacobi, who were generally on the side of the angels, but also with such protagonists of the Enlightenment as Lessing and Moses Mendelssohn, even with Nicolai, whom, as the editor of a liberal review, he regarded as the leader of "the blind Nicolaitans of Berlin." Goethe, who professed that he was a non-Christian and preferred therefore to have no personal contact with a man so decisively a Christian as was H., expressed nevertheless the highest admiration for his genius. He says of him in *Dichtung und Wahrheit,* "his *Socratic Memorabilia* attracted attention and were dear especially to those who could not bear the blinding light of the *Zeitgeist.* Here one divines a profound and solid thinker, who, though he was thoroughly acquainted with the contemporary world and its literature, was aware of something secret and inscrutable, which he expressed in his peculiar way. It is true that by the arbiters of literary fashion he was regarded as an abstruse fanatic; but young men eager in the pursuit of truth were drawn to him naturally. . . . I possess a collection of his works which is all but complete, and I have in manuscript a very important essay prompted by Herder's prize composition on the origin of speech, in which he throws marvelous flashes of light upon Herder's theory. I do not give up hope of an edition of Hamann's collected works, whether produced by me or at my instigation. And when this important document is available to the public it will be time to write about the author."

When Goethe visited Naples in 1787, his attention was called to a book by a writer of the previous century, Giambattista Vico, and to the friend who lent him the book he wrote, "With a hasty glance at the volume you loaned me as a sacred treasure I see that it contains Sibylic presentiments of the good and the right which some day will or ought to be realized, founded as they are upon earnest consideration of tradition and life. It is good for a nation to possess such an ancestor. The German people will some day find in Hamann a similar codex." Goethe sought to show that the original style of H.'s writing might be traced to a principle which he himself often asserted: "Everything a man attempts to perform, whether in deed or in word or in any other way, must spring from all his powers in unison. Whatever is dismembered is contemptible." This does indeed express the principle which H. consciously followed and which he called *lex continui*, meaning something very much like Kierkegaard's "reduplication."

Yet Goethe was diffident. "A fine maxim," said he, "but difficult to follow. It may be applied in life and in art; but in any communication by means of words it encounters a great difficulty. For in order to say something which has significance, the word must separate itself. In the fact that he speaks a man must for a moment be onesided; there is no communication, no teaching, without separation. Since Hamann, however, recoils from this separation once and for all, since he himself experienced, imagined and thought in a unity, therefore wished to speak in this way and required the same of others, he came with his original style into conflict with all that the others were capable of producing. To accomplish the impossible, he grasped at the primordial elements: with him profound and secret intuitions meet in hidden places together with moving utterances from sacred and profane authors, with illuminating flashes of understanding struck out by such an encounter, with whatever else of a humorous character there may be added—all this constitutes in its entirety the marvelous style of his communication. If one is unable to join him in the depths or to wander with him on the heights, if one cannot grasp the figures which hover before his eyes, and cannot discover the meaning of a passage barely suggested which he has drawn from the limitless literature at his command, one becomes the more troubled and darkened the more one studies him. I have in my collection some of his printed works in which with his own hand he has indicated on the margin the origin of the passages to which he alludes. On turning to them one finds again a dubious ambiguity which make a highly agreeable impression—but one must give up trying to *understand* in the ordinary sense of that word.[6] Such pas-

[6] The meaning of this phrase is explained by the concluding passage of a letter to Frau von Stein which Goethe wrote on Sept. 17, 1784, from the Court of Braunschweig and in the language, not too familiar to him, which was used in that court. "Haman de Konigsberg a ecrit une petite brochure contre le traité de Mendelssohn, qui a pour titre Jerusalem. J'ai toujours aimé les feuilles Sybellines de ce Mage modern et cette nouvelle production m'a fait un plaisir bien grand

sages deserve to be called Sibylistic for the further reason that they do not reveal at once their full meaning: one must wait for a favorable opportunity to appeal to these oracles. Each time one turns these pages one expects to find something new, because the meaning enshrined in every passage affects us at different times in different ways."

I do not grudge the space I give to this long quotation in what I hoped would be a short account of H.'s life; for Goethe gives a good account of the peculiarity of H.'s style and indicates the quality of his thinking which I have called "existential."

One might suppose that an author so highly acclaimed by Goethe would have been enriched by his writings. But, in fact, the age of Enlightenment could not boast of many readers, and therefore not even popular authors could expect to earn much by their pens. As for H., he ostentatiously shunned popularity; and though publishers as well as editors of reviews were eager to print whatever he wrote, they paid him nothing. At this H. made no complaint, for he recognized that "publishers have to live and cannot live on ether." Kantner, the one publisher in Königsberg, evidently did not live too well by his trade, for he cheerfully gave it up to take charge of a paper mill. At one time he persuaded H. to edit the only newspaper in Königsberg, and I supposed he must have been paid for that work—until I saw the statement that this paper had only two hundred subscribers. When there was no longer a publisher in their own town, H. as well as Kant had to rely on Hartnoch, a publisher in Riga. This man became an intimate friend and a frequent correspondent. I see mention of frequent gifts of salmon and caviar—but he paid his friend no royalties. Yet Hartnoch was so far from being niggardly that once he offered H. a large sum to pay for the education of his eldest daughter.

This offer was made at a time when H. felt free to decline it; for at the end of the year 1784 he received from an unknown admirer "a princely gift" designed expressly for the education of his four children. This gift which signally vindicated his faith in Providence and freed him for the rest of his life from financial distress came from Franz Buchholtz, a wealthy landholder in Westphalia, who had an ardent admiration for his writings and was distressed to learn that the author was financially embarrassed. He begged H. to regard him as a son, and proposed to visit him in Königsberg. H. had to tell this "dearly longed-for son" that his home was no place for

---

que je voudrais pouvoir partager avec toi, ce que sera difficile a cause de la matière et de façon dont il l'a traité. Il y a des bonmots impaiables et de tournures très serieuses, qui m'ont fait rire presque a chaque page. Apresant il faut que je relire le livre de Mendelssohn, pour mieux entendre son aversaire, car il m'a été impossible la première fois de la suivre toujours. Je me trouve très heureux d'avoir le sens, qu'il faut pour entendre jusqu'a un certain point les idées de ce tête unique, car on peut bien affirmer la paradox qu'on ne l'entend pas par l'entendement."

such a guest, but that he ardently desired to visit his benefactor in Munster. This fond project was deferred for two years because every request for leave of absence from the tax offices was refused, and when finally it was granted it amounted to dismissal with a small pension.

However humiliating these terms were, H. rejoiced in his liberation from a hated yoke. He had another reason for visiting Munster; for the Princess Gallitzin, one of the most brilliant women of her time, was living in that town and had a great desire to see him. Her admiration for his writings so piqued her curiosity about the man that she asked one of her acquaintances, Countess Kaiserling, to tell all she knew about him. For this reason the Count and Countess Kaiserling, who represented the most distinguished noble house in Königsberg, made a visit to H. in his kitchen and required him to lunch with them in their castle. It happened also that his dear friend Jacobi, then a widower, was living with his two sisters at Pempelfort, not far from Munster.

At last, in June 1787, when his health was already so much impaired that a long journey was dangerous, H. set out from Königsberg with his son Hans Michael. In Berlin he remained for some time with his friend Richart the composer. For the rest of the journey he was accompanied by his friend L. E. Lindner, who after being a tutor in Courland had become a physician and was one of the most distinguished physicians in Berlin. This "Doctor Rafael," as H. called him in allusion to the angel who accompanied Tobias, was good enough to attend him for a long while in Munster, though he never shared the Christian faith of his friend.

Nothing could exceed the kindness showed to the old and ailing man both in Pempelfort and in Munster. He shone in the brilliant company which frequented the house of Princess Gallitzin. Herder and Jacobi were there sometimes, but the company was predominantly Catholic. His benefactor Buchholtz was a Catholic. So too was the Princess Gallitzin, though she affirmed that only when she heard H. talk about the Bible did the scales fall from her eyes. Furstenberg as Prime Minister of Westphalia had done much to elevate the character of Catholicism in that state. He was often with the Princess; Hemsterhuis, a liberal Catholic author, was constantly in her suite; and Catholic clergymen were often guests in her house.

As a Lutheran, H. had been accustomed to speak about Romanism and the Papacy in a vulgar tone of disparagement, and he was astonished at the company he found at Munster. Never before had he known so many kindred spirits. It was "a foretaste of heaven," he said. There was of course talk about the possibility of his becoming a Catholic. But a letter of his to the Princess suggested tactfully that he was not inclined to change his ways. "Without placing dependence," he said, "upon principles which rest for the most part upon prejudices of our time, and without disdaining them, since they belong to the elements of this present world and our connection with it, surely the most certain ground of all peace is to be content with the pure milk of the Gospel and with the light given not by man but by God, which shines upon us in a dark place till the day shall dawn and the morning star arise—casting all our care upon *him* who has promised to care for us and our dear ones, relying upon the only Mediator and Advocate, whose blood speaks better things than that of Abel the first saint and martyr, and who has redeemed us from the vain conversation of our fathers. This is the alpha and omega of my philosophy: more than this I do not know and do not wish to know." But perhaps he expressed his position as clearly and more wittily when he reported that when he was on the point of leaving Wellbergen, the country estate of Buchholtz where he had gone to enjoy a period of solitude and repose before starting on the journey back to Königsberg, he had the chapel opened so that he might enter it to say "a good German Lutheran *Pater noster*."

He did not leave Wellbergen alive; for when Buchholtz and his wife came to escort him on the first stage of his journey, the physicians declared that he was too weak to travel. In fact, he died at 7 o'clock the following morning. Furstenberg and Buchholtz laid his body in the coffin. The Catholic clergy proposed to bury him in their cemetery; but the Princess insisted that he be buried in her garden, and Hemsterhuis composed the inscription on his monument: the monogram of Christ, followed by an appropriate text taken from the Vulgate (I Cor. 1:23, 27), and the dedication: *Johanni Georgio Hamanni, viro Christiano*.

II.

AN ACCOUNT OF SOME OF HIS WRITINGS

All of H.'s writings were prompted by intellectual occurrences, some of which may seem to us no more important than straws. In apology for this he cited the words of Hamlet:

> 'Tis not to be great
> Never to stir without great argument;
> But greatly to find quarrel in a straw
> When honor is at stake.

But from the brief sketch of H.'s life already given one can see that the *Socratic Memorabilia*, which H. regarded as the beginning of his "authorship," was not prompted by a trivial circumstance. He had been tried almost beyond endurance by the persistent efforts of his bosom friend Christoph Berens to convert him by his letters to an appreciation of the Enlightenment, and the climax of his exasperation was reached when Berens was obliged to come to

Königsberg to rescue his younger brother George from the dissolute life he was leading in the university. Berens could not forget that his old friend was another lost sheep whom he still might hope to save. The breach between these two men was already so deep that they met without any show of affection. But Berens had become intimate with Kant, and he persuaded the Professor to join him on a visit to H. in the hope that so great a philosopher might be able to change the mind of this obdurate man. Since the first visit bore no obvious fruit, these persistent apostles proposed to repeat the visit. H. begged to be excused from a second attempt to convert him, and his answer to the "two" was the *Socratic Memorabilia*, which was preceded by a personal letter to Kant.

It was not by casual choice he took Socrates as his theme; for, though he did not then know the Socratic literature so thoroughly as he did later, this simple old Greek philosopher was so congenial to him that he claimed he could have written half the dialogues of Plato before he had read them. These two men, in fact, were so alike in their life and thought that it was not unreasonable of H. to single out, as he did in this book, the most striking points of resemblance—especially the fact that the way of life in the case of both men corresponded to their philosophy, this being one aspect of the *lex continui*, which Kierkegaard called "reduplication."

The title page of this book, as of all H.'s publications, was meant to be a cryptic indication of its contents: "a promissory note which is to be paid in full by what follows."

SOCRATIC MEMORABILIA

For the Lange Weile [boredom] of the Public
Compiled by
A Lover of Lange Weile [leisure]
With a Double Dedication:
To Nobody and to Two.

In his favorite Latin writer, Persius, H. found four lines which seem to justify this double dedication, and he quoted them at the bottom of the title page. I translate here only the words which are significant in this connection: "Who reads such a thing?"—"Perhaps two, perhaps nobody." At the foot of the page Amsterdam is named as the place of publication, and 1759 as the year, without indicating the name of the publisher. In fact, this booklet was printed in Halle (taken there by an agent who died on the journey, so that H. lost track of his production), and because the local censor condemned as pernicious a book which he could not understand, the publisher had to resort to the fiction that it was published in Holland.

Although this book was written for two men, Berens and Kant, it was also dedicated, with more reason than Kant was able to see, to the great Public, here described as "Nobody, the Notorious." For, in fact, this "Nobody" upon which H. heaped his scorn, as Kierkegaard did upon "the Crowd," was the idol secretly worshipped by Berens and Kant, along with all the leaders of the *Aufklärung*; and these two friends of his were conspiring to "seduce" him to take part in this idolatry by becoming an author and writing in a way that would be pleasing to the Public. They succeeded, ironically enough, in prompting him to become an author, but his whole authorship was a protest against their idolatry. Like Naaman the Syrian, when he had been cleansed of his leprosy by bathing in the Jordan, H. felt free to bow in the temple of Rimmon; but in the two pages he dedicated to the Public he did not disguise the contempt he felt for the idol and for the vanity of its worshippers.

Kant had reproached him for "pride" in scorning the prevailing opinion of his age. To this he replied in a letter to the Magister: "I almost have to laugh at the choice of a philosopher as the means of bringing about in me a change of mind. I take the best demonstration no more seriously than a sensible girl does a love letter. Not your say, not mine counts; not your reason, not mine—that is to compare one watch with another, but only the sun keeps the right time. You cannot convince me, for I am not one of your hearers, but an accuser and an opponent. I am disposed to be patient with you so long as I can hope to win you, and to be weak because you are weak. You must inquire of me, not of yourself, if you wish to understand me. . . . Shall I not burn if someone is offended in me? and for what? because of my pride. I tell you, you must learn to experience this pride, or at least to imitate it, even to excel it—or else you must choose my humility as a pattern and renounce the lust of authorship. Or prove to me that your vanity is better than the pride which offends you and the humility which you despise. Either you must rise to my pride or I must stoop to your vanity."

It is astonishing that Kant could listen to such candid talk without being roused to anger. But between these two men, who represented opposite poles of thought, there never occurred, so far as we know, the slightest rift. We are surprised to learn that at this time Kant asked H. to coöperate with him in writing a book of physics for schools, meaning by this an account of the visible universe. With regard to this H. wrote "Two Love Letters with a Supplement addressed to a Teacher of World-Wisdom who wanted to write a physics for children." The two men were unable to agree upon a plan because Kant's "vanity" inhibited him from writing in the language of children—"as the proud Creator of the world did when he wrote the story of the Creation." "The proud Author and Ruler of the world knew that his plan was good, whatever others might think of it. But if God should hear the Public clapping their hands and stamping their feet to express approval of this best of worlds, he would turn to the angels who surround him, covering their feet as well as their eyes, and would ask them if perhaps he had said something foolish when he said, 'Let there be light'—like the tyrant Phocian who, when the crowd applauded something he had said, asked his friends if he had happened to say something especially stupid."

In the dedication to the Public "the two" are described without mention of their names. One of them (Berens) is said to be engaged in the search for the philosophers' stone, as a philanthropist who regards gold as the means for accomplishing the greatest good of the greatest number. The other (Kant) is an exponent of universal world-wisdom, who might serve like Newton as Warden of the Mint—but, alas, criticism is not able to eradicate the spurious thoughts which have crept into our books, as the surer criticism of chemistry insures the purity of silver and gold.

This little book, he tells the public, is not sweetened like a cake which has to be chewed, for in fact it is a pill which has to be swallowed. It is like the big pill of pitch which Daniel made for Bel the Dragon and thereby caused him to burst asunder. He hopes that a couple of these pills will be left over to purge "the two" of their superstition.

The dedication to "the two" is more flattering. It begins by remarking that "the public in Greece read Aristotle's treatise on the Natural History of Animals—and Alexander understood it." In fact, Aristotle said of this work, as H. might say of his, that "it was just the same as not published." But H. expects his two friends to understand him—as Alexander alone understood Aristotle. He says in conclusion, "Since you are both my friends, your partisan praise and your partisan blame will be equally acceptable to me." But he warns them that they "must be able to swim." He claims that in writing about Socrates he is writing in a Socratic manner: "*Analogy* was the soul of his argumentation, and to this he gave *irony* for its body." If they think that the confidence with which he writes is incompatible with the ignorance he professes, they may ascribe this to imitation of Socrates. Socrates was confident of what he learned from his daemon—and H. too could rely upon divine oracles. "Socrates, my dear Sirs, was no common critic. He distinguished in the writings of Heraclitus between what he understood and what he did not understand, and he drew very reasonable and modest inferences from the comprehensible to the incomprehensible."

The Introduction, of approximately four pages, challenges the fashion of regarding the history of philosophy as a lifeless monument. H. would do better than that in dealing with Socrates. "A statue was erected in honor of a French minister of state, carved by the chisel of a celebrated sculptor, at the expense of a monarch who gave his name to a century and gazed with admiration at the marble image of his great subject—whereas only the Sythian who travelled as an apprentice and was a *carpenter* like Noah and like him whom the fanciful Julian called the Galilaean—this Sythian, in order to become the god of his people, committed an indiscretion, the memory of which might alone be sufficient to eternalize him: he ran up to the marble and magnanimously offered the dumb stone the half of his kingdom, if he would teach him how to govern the other half. This is worthy of becoming a legend, like that of Pygmalion the sculptor of his wife, who fell so in love with the work of his hands that he begged the gods to give it life." This is H.'s way of saying that he proposes to vivify the picture of Socrates. One might say more prosaically that both Girardon the sculptor of the monument to Richelieu and Louis XIV who caused it to be erected regarded it only as stone—until a Russian, Peter the Great, addressed it as a living being.

"In the Temple of Learning there is an idol called History of Philosophy, which has no lack of Levites and priests devoted to its service." At this point H. indulges in a sharp criticism of the most recent historians of philosophy in French, English, and German, who treat it as a *corpus vile;* and also of the contemporary philosophers who make a poor use of the gallery of dead statues furnished by the historians, without sensing the life which pulses in them. Aesop and La Fontaine, though they were men of no great intellectual power, and had no share in the nature of the beasts they describe, were able to reproduce their thoughts with lively sympathy. By such men the history of philosophy might be well served. Perhaps "a bit of fanaticism and superstition" (for which H. was reproached by his two friends) may be needed in order to ferment in the soul a philosophic heroism, a burning ambition for truth and virtue, and the courage to overcome lies and vices. This is the heroic spirit of the true teacher of world-wisdom, which will enable him to perceive that the cloud of witnesses that surrounds us comprises divine men from among the heathen, whom heaven has anointed as messengers and interpreters and has consecrated to the same calling that the prophets had among the Jews. As nature was given us to open our eyes, so was history to open our ears. To dissect to its primal elements each body and each event is to take God by surprise, even his eternal power and Godhead. Therefore one who has not Moses and the Prophets will be, though against his will and without his knowledge, only a poet, as was Buffon in his history of creation, and Montesquieu in his history of the Roman Empire. Would not the artist who was able to pass a lentil through a needle's eye have enough lentils to practice his dexterity if you gave him a bushel? In spite of the destruction of the library at Alexandria and others like it, we have enough books for the practice of profitless proficiency. Let no one think that juggling with technical terms is philosophy. I wonder that no one has yet ventured to do for history what Bacon did for physics by taking God's Book for his guide. It is obvious to human reason that, if God's providence is not operative everywhere, so that no sparrow falls to the ground without our Father, it can be effective nowhere. Bollingbroke counselled his students to regard the whole of ancient history as a revelation of pagan theology and as a poetic dictionary. But perhaps all history has more the nature of mythology than this philosopher thought, and like nature is a sealed book, a hidden testimony, a riddle, which can be solved only by ploughing with another heifer than our reason.

These are H.'s words, not mine. I hesitate to include them in inverted commas only because I have omitted enough to make it possible for one to read without tears.

H. did not propose to write a life of Socrates, but to dwell only upon the memorabilia which were pertinent to the situation in his time, thus giving an example of the way the history of philosophy ought to be treated. He refers to the story that Socrates often visited the workshop of his simple friend Simon (called here "the tanner" in allusion to Peter's host at Joppa), and that this man it was who first thought of recording the philosopher's sayings—and perhaps did it with more understanding than Plato. "If only I can understand my hero as well as did Simon the tanner!"

The first section of this little book compares the Socratic wisdom with the Christian truth which excels it. Socrates thought it significant that his mother was a midwife; for like her he assumed the humble role of bringing ideas to birth in his pupils and did not claim to create them. Although this saying of his has often been repeated, it has not really been understood by a modern generation of Athenians, who are not content to accept truth as something given but are proud of discovering or creating it. It is no less significant that his father was a sculptor. From him he learned to appreciate the beauty of the human form, believing too fondly that to a beautiful body there must correspond a beautiful soul; and, alas, by this he was led into behavior which even in a pagan was discreditable. He himself was no mean sculptor, for in Athens a monument to the Three Graces was attributed to him; and it is characteristic of him that, in contradiction to the newer theology, he depicted these goddesses fully clothed, as the ancient tradition required. Socrates was not a man who presumed to behold naked truth. It is the peculiarity of sculptural art that the artist accomplishes his purpose by hewing away from the wood or the stone everything which hides the true image he sees with the mind's eye.

The falsehoods which result from human indolence, and from the pride which is only apparently its opposite, Socrates resolutely hewed away, and therefore his contemporaries complained that he had reduced the oaks of their forests to shavings and their rocks to splinters. Those who in our day exalt the son of the sculptor at the expense of the son of the carpenter can find in Socrates' words witnesses against them. Angered by the Christian criticism which reduces their proud constructions to splinters, these modern Athenians prove themselves true sons of their fathers who prepared the poison for Socrates. They cannot endure the contradiction that one who was promised as a saviour, fairer than all the children of men, should turn out to be a man of sorrows, full of wounds and stripes—the scandal of the Cross. We find a like contradiction in the oracle of Delphi which indicated that Socrates, who professed to know nothing, was the wisest of men.

The second section recounts that a man named Criton, who had money to spend, and evidently knew how to spend it, undertook to transform Socrates from a sculptor into a sophist. In spite of the many teachers who were provided by this man's liberality, Socrates remained "ignorant." There are several ways of understanding his claim to ignorance—about which he seems to have talked as much as a hypochondriac does of his imaginary ailments. To understand what it means, one must have a sympathetic experience of it. *Know thyself* was the inscription everyone read who entered the temple at Delphi, and all knew it by rote, though they did not understand it. When the question was asked of Apollo, "Who is the wisest man?" one might expect that the reply would point to Sophocles or Euripides; for these men could not become such eminent tragedians as they were, if they had not been skillful in dissecting the hearts of men. But Socrates excelled them because he had gone further than they in self-knowledge, having probed deeply into his own heart and learned that he knew nothing. It was because of his conversion and his experience of self-knowledge as a descent into hell that H. was able to perceive a connection which Plato failed to see between the famous motto of the temple at Delphi and the oracle which pronounced Socrates the wisest of men. H. understood that the fear of God is the beginning of wisdom; for in his conversion he learned not only the depravity of the human heart but the impotence of human reason. So it is he had "a sympathetic understanding" of the Socratic ignorance. He understood that this was not the affected ignorance of the skeptical philosophers which leads to disbelief in everything except the ambitious structures which they themselves have erected upon their doubt, but that it was an ignorance which leads to faith.

"I know no more venerable seal (which at the same time is a key) to the testimony Socrates gave of his ignorance than the oracle pronounced by the great teacher of the Gentiles (1 Cor. 8:2): 'If any man thinketh that he knoweth anything, he knoweth not yet as he ought to know; but if any man loveth God, the same is known of God.' The fact, however, that our natural wisdom, like a grain of corn, must decay, pass into ignorance, and that out of this *nothing* the life and substance of a higher knowledge must germinate, is a truth into which the nose of a sophist is not long enough to pry."

"What is it in Homer that compensates for his ignorance of those rules of art which Aristotle deduced from his works? And what is it in Shakespeare that compensates for his ignorance or violation of the critical laws? Genius, is the unanimous answer. Socrates then could well afford to be ignorant, for he had a genius or daemon on which he could rely, whom he loved and feared as his God, whose *peace* was more to him than all the reason of the Egyptians and the Greeks, whose voice also he *believed*. From the ignorance of Socrates flow naturally the peculiarities of his way of teaching and thinking. Nothing could be more natural than that he should always feel compelled to ask in order to become wise; that he should be credulous, accepting every opinion as true, and should prefer to treat it humorously and jestingly rather than to enter into a serious investigation; that he drew all his arguments from sensible apprehensions and from analogy; that he uttered apophthegms because he knew no dialectic, was indifferent to what people call the truth, had also no passions, least of all such as the noblest among the Athenians knew well, that, like all *idiotes*, he often spoke as confidently and decisively, as if of all the owls of his fatherland it was he alone that sat upon the helmet of Minerva."

It is evident that here H. describes himself as well as Socrates, especially with regard to the contradiction between ignorance and confidence. For H. too had oracles upon which he relied.

He affirms that, if he possessed the talent of the historians who are able to resuscitate a buried age and out of the ashes of a deceased hero effect a palingenesis, he could paint a picture of the country and the city in which Socrates lived in order to show how aptly his ignorance was calculated for the conditions of his people and of his age, as well as for the special business of his life. "The Athenians were inquisitive. An ignorant man is the best physician for this disease of concupiscence. Like all inquisitive persons they were inclined to communicate their thoughts, so it must have pleased them to be asked questions. They possessed, however, more talent for discovery and exposition than for retention and judgment. Hence Socrates had always an opportunity to come to the aid of their memory and judgment and to warn them against frivolity and vanity. In short, Socrates enticed his fellow countrymen out of the labyrinth created by their learned sophists to *a truth which lies in the hidden parts, to a heavenly wisdom,* and from the idolatrous altars of their zealous and worldly-wise priests to the service of *an unknown God."* Thus H. describes the "Athenians" of his day.

In the third section, which is the last, we have a brief sketch of the principal traits exhibited by Socrates in relation to his contemporaries. We may note that these were also the traits of H., and that the Athenians of Socrates' day were not unlike the "Athenians" of the eighteenth century. It is said here that Socrates was a patriotic citizen, who had fought in three wars against the Persians. In the first war he had saved the life of Alcibiades, in the second that of his friend Xenophon, and from the defeat of the third war he escaped, as he did also from the pest which twice in his lifetime raged in Athens. But reverence for the word within his own heart, to which he was always attentive, excused him from attending town meetings; and when at a certain age he accepted a position on the city council, his awkwardness in counting the vote made him ridiculous, and his stubbornness in resisting what seemed to him injustice subjected him to the suspicion of being a revolutionary.

"Socrates never became an author, and in this he was self-consistent. Like the hero of the battle of Marathon, who needed no children to keep his name in remembrance, Socrates needed no books to serve as his monument. His philosophy was suitable to every place and to every occasion. The market, the field, a banquet, served as his schoolroom, and he availed himself of every circumstance of human life for sowing the seeds of truth. Though he could be reproached with no pedantry, and could entertain the best company, even if it was composed of rude young men, it is also said that for whole days and nights he stood immovable, more like one of his statues than like himself. Perhaps his books, if he had written them, would have been as enigmatical as these soliloquies. For no one knew the real Socrates.

"Perhaps at home he lacked the repose, the quiet, the cheer, which a philosopher needs for writing—although the tales told about Xanthippe are for the most part inventions. He was irritable, and she naturally was irritated. His hot temper, it is said, prompted him sometimes to tear his hair in the market place. But were there not priests and sophists enough in Athens to account for Socrates' rage? Was not the meek and gentle Teacher of mankind compelled to pronounce a series of woes against the learned and pious leaders of the people?

"Compared with Xenophon and Plato, the style of Socrates perhaps suggested the chisel of the sculptor, and his way of speaking was rather plastic than pictorial. An example of this is the prognostication of his condemnation which appears in the comparison he made between himself and a physician who forbade children to eat cakes and candy. Such a man would surely be condemned to death, if the children were his judges. In fact, it was from sweetmeats Socrates tried to wean his fellow countrymen. Socrates was charged with neglecting the gods and with seducing young men by his free and offensive teaching. He replied to these charges with such earnestness and courage, with such pride and coolness, that he seemed rather like the judge of his judges than a culprit dependent upon their commiseration.

"Plato regards the voluntary poverty of Socrates as a sign of his divine calling. A greater sign is the fact that he shared the fate of prophets and righteous men (Matt. 23:29). A statue by Lysippus was the monument the Athenians erected to attest his innocence and the injustice of their condemnation of him."

The brief Conclusion can be translated here almost in its entirety. "One who does not know how to live on crusts and alms, nor by robbery, and is not ready to sell everything for a sword, is not cut out to be a servant of the truth. Rather let him be a serviceable and efficient man of the world, or learn how to bow and scrape and lick plates—then he will be safe all his life long from hunger and thirst, from the gallows and from the torture wheel. It is true that God himself, according to the good confession he made before Pilate—it is true, I say, that God himself became a man and to this end entered into the world that he might bear witness unto the truth. So no omniscience was needed to foresee that he would not get off so easily as Socrates but would die by a crueler and more shameful death."

Having devoted so much space to a little book of only thirty-two pages (or "four sheets octavo," as H. reckoned), it is only too evident that at this rate we shall not be able to describe in a single essay all of H.'s works, short as they are, but must be content to mention a few samples and to describe them with stricter parsimony in the use of words.

I give a brief description of the *Clouds*, which is a companion to the *Memorabilia* and a book of the same size, published a year later as a reply to a contemptuous review in the *Hamburger Nachrichten* ("from the realm of learning"). The title was obviously chosen to recall the comedy in which Aristophanes made fun of Socrates, and the book is full of Aristophanian wit. Writing anonymously, H. pretends to agree with the criticism of the reviewer, but ironically he is heaping scorn upon his critic. This is a serious book, though it bubbles with humor. The notes announced on the title page (*cum notis variorum in usum Delphini*) are devoted to a sharp criticism of the critic. The page which follows them has an apt motto taken from Job 34:7, written both in Hebrew and in Latin, which in our translation reads: "What man is like Job, who drinketh up scorning like water." In these words H. described himself. The comedy which follows in three acts is introduced by the words of Hamlet:

The play's the thing
Wherein I'll catch the conscience of the King.

The humor becomes most exuberant in Act Third, which ends, however, on a very serious note. An abrupt transition like this was characteristic of H. He alludes to this trait in a letter to Kant: "At one moment I am a leviathan, monarch and prime minister of the ocean, from whose breath its ebb and flow depend. The next moment I seem to myself a whale, which, as said the great poet (Ps. 104:26), God made to deport himself in the sea."

This act begins by appraising the opinion of the reviewer that the author of the *Memorabilia* must be a madman, crazed by a madness which, judging by several favorable reviews of the book, appears to be infectious. H. considers the question how genius is related to madness. This is a question which preoccupied Kierkegaard, and it is likely that he drew upon the mass of erudition which H. accumulated at this point. We see from a letter to Lindner that H. was satisfied with this book. "The *Clouds* are just what they ought to be. Inspiration and erudition are two proud steeds, two stallions, which I here drive as a team. Art cannot be carried further—or, if one would regard it in this way, genius cannot be more unbridled than I suffer it to be here. To unite such opposites is not in every man's power." He says in the *Clouds*, "Hippolytus, in spite of all the pains he took to eliminate the element of divinity (τό θεῖον), which he regarded as the obstacle to his art, was at the conclusion of his book on the Sacred Sickness compelled nevertheless to admit the new principle: All is divine, and all is human too (πάντα θεῖα καὶ ἀνθρώπινα πάντα)."

In conclusion H. addresses his muse: "O wondrous Muse, who teachest a man to pipe where no one is willing to dance, who promptest him to wail where no one will mourn, because thy readers are like children sitting in the marketplace! Wondrous Muse, show me the youth who shall rebuke the scribes of our day who possess the key of knowledge, but do not enter themselves and who hinder those who are entering in. Show me the youth for whom the fierce camel provides clothing, who dips his rod in wild honey so that his eyes are enlightened (I Sam. 14:27). Delighted to hear the voice of the bridegroom, he stands and listens, for he is a friend. For he who has the bride is the Bridegroom. The office of philosophy is represented by Moses in person, a schoolmaster to lead us to faith; and unto this day, in all the schools where it is read, there is a veil upon the hearts of the teachers and hearers, which veil is done away in

Christ. This is the true light which we do not see by the light of common sense, nor in the light of the tutelary genius. Lo, he comes upon the clouds! Where the Lord is the Spirit, there is freedom. But we all, with unveiled face, reflecting as in a mirror the glory of the Lord, are transformed into the same image from glory to glory, even as from the Lord the Spirit (II Cor. 3:18)."

In 1762 twelve short works by H., most of which had already appeared in magazines, were published by Kantner in one volume entitled *Crusades of the Philologian*. The word crusade indicates aptly the character of these articles; for they were obviously militant and bore conspicuously the sign of the Cross. The militant purpose was indicated by the motto on the title page:

> *Erunt etiam altera bella,*
> *Atque iterum ad Troiam magnus mittetur*
> *Achilles.*

Also by the Hebrew line on the following page quoted from Eccles. 12:11, "The words of the wise are goads." What H. understood by the word philologian is not at once so evident. In claiming to be a philologian he did not mean to put himself on a level with the learned lexicographers of his day; for his interest in speech lay deeper than theirs, although he made diligent use of their works and sought to improve them. In the etymological sense of the word, a philologian is a lover of the logos. H. thought first of all of the divine Logos through whom God spoke and revealed himself at the Creation, most evidently in the word, "Let there be light"; in the creation of man in his own image; in human history; and in the Scriptures, which is the Author's own interpretation of his words and works. And surely the Author must be the best interpreter of his own words. In the second place, logos is the speech by which man reveals himself to man. It is a product of human reason, indeed it is reason itself made audible and visible. H. once wrote to Herder, "If I were as eloquent as Demosthenes, I still should have to utter only one word, thrice repeated: Reason is speech, logos. On this marrowbone I gnaw, and likely I shall continue to gnaw myself to death. For me darkness still obscures this deep; I am always waiting for an apocalyptic angel bearing a key to this abyss."

Not all the articles in this book are of equal worth. I mention here only two of them. The *Clover Leaf of Hellenic Letters* is accounted one of the best. But I need only refer to it because the most important features recur in *Aesthetics in a Nutshell*. By many of his admirers this little work is singled out as the most perfect thing he ever wrote. Of course, it is not easy to understand; but it has been said that every way it is turned a new light breaks out from it, as from a well-cut diamond. "A nutshell" suggests the brevity of this piece, but one may be sure it was not the only suggestion the author intended to convey. He expected that many who saw the shell would not find the kernel. For about aesthetics he had something to say far more profound than the philosophers commonly understand; and what he says here, though it was written before Kant dealt with this subject, may be regarded as a criticism of this philosopher's subsequent work.

He called this little book "A Rhapsody in Cabalistic Prose." To explain what he meant by cabalistic would lead us too far afield; but we may note that the rhapsodists were the interpreters of the Homeric poems, and H. essays here to interpret the works of the Poet who in the beginning revealed himself as the Author of the world. Poetry is the mother tongue of mankind. First came the poets, and after them the philosophers, who sought by their theories of aesthetics to understand their art. However plain God's speech is, some homogeneity is required in order to understand it. The crown of God's creation is man, whom he made in his own image. With this the poesy of the Ancient of Days became dramatic instead of epic. Speech is translation from the language of angels into the language of men: thoughts become words, things become names, pictures become signs. A translation, as the third of the Hellenistic Letters remarks, is always inferior to the original. It is like seeing the design of a tapestry from the back. The original can be apprehended only by one who knows the language thoroughly; hence the torch of Moses (the light of divine revelation) is necessary for a genuine scientific understanding. A merely human understanding may be reached by dissection and analysis, but it does not comprehend the real nature of man. Beauty is discoverable only when every creature is rightly referred to its Source.

"Through philosophical *abstractions* the text of nature is more thoroughly corrupted than by all the myths and fables that have ever been spun." "O for a muse like a refiner's fire and like fuller's soap which will cleanse away all the abstractions whereby our concepts of things are as thoroughly mutilated as the Creator is suppressed and blasphemed. I speak to you, Greeks, because you think yourselves wiser. Make the attempt to read the *Iliad* after you have sifted out by abstraction the two vowels alpha and omega, and tell me what is your opinion of the intelligence and euphony of the poet." "Do not venture to deal with the metaphysics of the fine arts before you are perfected in the Eleusinian orgies and mysteries. For to Ceres belong the senses, and the passions to Bacchus." "Apart from the senses and the passions, which philosophers ignore, there is no truth and no beauty. One can indeed be a man without being an author; but the notion that one might conceive of an author without thinking of him as a man is an abstraction more poetic than philosophical." "If, as Voltaire thinks, our theology is not worth as much as mythology, it is utterly impossible for us to equal, not to say surpass, the poetry of the pagans. If our poetry is worthless, our history, which leaves out God, seems thinner than Pharaoh's lean kine. About our philosophy it is needless to speak—cobwebs in a ruined castle. Every sluggard who knows only a little kitchen Latin and Swiss-German, but whose name is stamped with the whole number M [*magister artium*] or the half number D [*doctor divinitatis*], which are the numbers of the Academic Beast, is authorized to demonstrate lies at which the benches and those who sit upon them must cry out in desperation, if the former had ears, and if the latter, who with jocular irony are called 'hearers,' were accustomed to hear with their ears."

What is to be done to bring the dead to life? Nothing is to be done by learning and scientific investigation. Bacon, in his *Consensum rerum universalium*, from which H. quotes at length, indicates a different way. But H. knows a way that is shorter: "The Lord himself must rend the heavens and come down to restore these dead bones to life. New stars must awaken new magi to ape the title of kings but to bring their treasures, gold and frankincense and myrrh, to the feet of the divine Child, to whom every knee shall bow, and every tongue confess that Jesus Christ is Lord, to the glory of God the Father."

I am tempted to say something about *A New Apology for the Letter "h"* which was published about a year later than the *Crusades*; for here is an instance where H. seems to fight about a straw but really was defending essential Christianity. What prompted him to write was a book by a man of not much consequence who announced himself as an ex-rector and extraordinary professor, and who, in the liberal spirit of his age, denounced the traditional forms of Christianity, and only incidentally advanced and defended the proposition that the letter "h" wherever it is silent in the middle of a word or at the end ought not to be written.

H. takes up the cudgels in defense of this poor little letter, as though he were interested only in a correct orthography. But he perceived that this simplified spelling was significant of the tendency of that time. "H" is hardly a consonant but only a breathing or *spiritus*; and the representatives of his age were intent upon eliminating spirit. With mordant wit and devastating satire, but with a show of pedantry which was appropriate to the "schoolmaster" to whom he attributed his little book, H. annihilated his inconspicuous opponent and "the blind Nicolaitans of Berlin" whom he might be supposed to represent. Then when the schoolmaster has to leave, with the excuse that three classes are waiting for him, the little letter "h" takes up his own defense with a vigor which could hardly be expected of one so small. He writes in the tone of the prophets of Israel against "the little prophets of Böhmisch-Breda."

Although scant space is left for the consideration of this author's works, I am loath to omit a brief reference to his criticism of Herder's prize essay on the origin of speech which was crowned by the Berlin Academy in 1772 and initiated his fame as an author. The question proposed by the Academy was whether speech is of divine or human origin. Herder dismissed what he called "the higher hypothesis" and decided for a human origin. It is not likely that his essay would have been crowned by such an academy, if the author had elected to defend the higher hypothesis. In fact, he made himself agreeable to his judges by speaking of the Biblical story of the Creation as "an oriental account." H. could not fail to perceive that his dear young friend, his Alcibiades, though he was a pious Lutheran pastor, was courting the *Zeitgeist*; and friendship did not restrain him from criticizing the prize essay—first in two reviews published in the *Königsberg Zeitung*, then in two brochures: (1) "The Last Will and Testament of the Knight of Rosenkreuz about the divine and human origin of speech"; (2) "Philological Aphorisms and Doubts about a prize essay on the question whether speech is of human or divine origin." In this last he ventures to express only his "doubts"—"because it would be highly ridiculous to attempt to disprove a truth which not only has been thoroughly proved but has also been crowned. I find myself therefore reduced to the agreeable necessity of offering the incense of doubt to the fashionable spirit of my century." In his first review he blurted out the accusation: "The author has the credit of attaining the prize of the Academy by his *disobedience*." What he meant by this is made evident by a milder sentence in one of his letters to Herder: "Your theme is happily chosen and provides always a wide field for an inquiring spirit—if one gives free rein to the imagination, but without therewith renouncing obedience, the analogy of the faith." (Our translation is "the proportion of faith.")

He charges that Herder had not so much proved the human origin as discarded the higher hypothesis—which nevertheless many of his remarks seem to justify. For his own part H. adopts no extravagant position but is content with the maxim Hippolytus found himself compelled to affirm: "All things are divine, and they are also human." Essentially this corresponds with the judgment passed upon this essay by Goethe, to whom when he was only twenty-one years of age the manuscript was submitted by the author. Writing about this many years later Goethe said, "The question seemed to me rather otiose; for if God created man as man, he must have created human speech as well as man's upright gait and the organs appropriate for vocalization. Of course from a naturalistic point of view everything seems human." Although this question was indeed otiose, the treatment it received from Herder needed to be rebuked. I recall that Ruskin in one of his supersensitive moments inveighed bitterly against a botanist who with a scientific simplicity of mind affirmed that plants exist for the purpose of producing seeds. This is a cheerless view which ignores the happy activity of the plant in producing with infinite cunning beautiful flowers and luscious fruits, an activity which evidently represents the climax of its individual life. The question as to what is the plant's chief end may seem as otiose as the question whether the egg or the hen came first; but upon the answer depends what Fechner called "the daylight view of the world."

I am happy to report that this controversy did not for a moment interrupt the friendship of these two men. Indeed, in his last and most forceful attack H. hailed Herder as "the most worthy of all my friends," and said, "I bequeath to him my joy and my crown (Phil. 4:11)"—meaning his two children, to whom Michael, his only son, Herder stood as godfather, expecting that, upon the death of the Magus, Herder would "give them bread and wine (Lam. 2:12)—and to me erect no monument of stone."

We started with the *Socratic Memorabilia*, which was Hamann's reply to Kant's vain effort to convert him; and now, having made a full circle, we come to what might be called his attempt to convert Kant, if he had seriously thought of anything so futile. The *Critique of Pure Reason* was published in 1781, when Kant, who was six years older than H. had been Professor of Philosophy for thirty-four years, having "set up his throne in Königsberg" in 1747. Hartnoch, who was their common publisher in Riga, sent the proofs of this book to H. without waiting to ask Kant's permission. H. devoured them with his customary voracity, and therefore as soon as the book was published he could send a review of it, on June 1, to the *Königsberger Zeitung*—which, however, he withdrew and "tabled." Not till three years later did he compose a more formal confutation of the fundamental principles upon which the Kantian philosophy was constructed, calling it "Metacritique of the Purism of the Pure Reason"—and this too he tabled.[7] As a reason for holding his criti-

[7] Professor Robert Scoon, of Princeton University, calls my attention to a conjecture made in 1918 by Professor Kemp Smith in his *Commentary to Kant's Critique of Pure Reason* (in the section on "Kant's Refutation of Idealism," pp. 305-315), to the effect that Hamann was one of the early critics (along with Pistorius and Garve) who succeeded in inducing Kant to alter radically in the 2nd ed. of the *Critique of Pure Reason* (1787) statements which in the 1st ed. verged upon the skepticism of Hume and went beyond the subjective idealism of Berkeley. It is plausible to suppose that in his frequent conversations with Kant H. may have found occasion to express his objections to the "rotten foundations"

cism he alleged that Kant was not only his friend but his benefactor. Yet in these critical reviews he had treated Kant with the utmost respect, and never before had he refrained from attacking his friends in the interest of truth, though from some of them he had received benefactions greater than he could attribute to Kant, who had only the merit of helping him to get the job by which he supported his family, and of permitting his son to hear his lectures without paying a fee. One may suspect that he was prompted by other considerations, perhaps by the feeling that he had not succeeded in formulating to his own satisfaction the objections he had in mind against the Critical Philosophy. He wrote to Herder, "The whole idea has miscarried, and I have thought of putting an end to the thing so that I might get the thought out of my mind." He did not succeed in getting this thought out of his mind; for till nearly the end of his life his letters dwelt frequently upon Kant and the oppositions he framed against the Kantian philosophy. No one recognized more promptly than H. the fundamental importance of Kant's first great work, which in fact has determined the course of subsequent philosophies, either by attraction or by repulsion. He was not dazzled by it, as were many of his contemporaries, like Mendelssohn and Nicolai; but he must have recognized that here was a giant who was not likely to be slain by a youth who chose a round stone from his scrip and slung it with his sling.

From what we already know of H. we can divine what sort of objections he would raise. They were existential objections like those which Kierkegaard raised against the subsequent forms of idealistic philosophy devised by Fichte and Hegel. First of all, he declared that what nature has joined together no man may put asunder, that tradition and experience cannot be separated from reason, and that reason may be made to seem "pure" only by a vain abstraction from relative as well as from absolute life, an abstraction which becomes fantastical when the reason is conceived of in three forms: the pure (theoretical), the practical, and the critical.

---

of the Critical Philosophy. It is certain that his influence would be exerted in the direction of realism. From the letters I have quoted it may be seen how candid he was with Kant and how zealous to "convert" him. We have seen that his two trenchant reviews of his friend's great work were not published, and it is not likely that the manuscripts were shown to "the Prussian Hume"; but from them we may infer what objections he must have expressed to Kant orally. They were fundamental objections, and nothing but a fundamental change in Kant's position would have satisfied him. His hope of converting him was based upon the high estimation in which he held him. He said of Kant in a letter to Herder, "Apart from the old Adam in his authorship, he is really an obliging and useful man, at bottom an unselfish and noble-minded man of high talent and merit." Writing to Hippel he said, "Kant, as even his enemies must admit, is one of our cleverest pates; but unfortunately this cleverness is his evil demon, very much as Lessing's is."

It is only by the co-operation of all man's faculties that true knowledge can be attained. "It is only the reason of the schools," he said in a letter to Jacobi, "which separates itself into idealism and realism. The true and genuine reason knows nothing of this fictitious distinction, which is not founded upon the nature of things and contradicts the unity which lies, or ought to lie, at the basis of all our conceptions." By pure reason Kant cannot discover the nature of the thing-in-itself but is content with appearances which are wholly subjective, and out of such airy material he builds his world. But tradition, whether it be in the form of faith or not, cannot reasonably be ignored—without Berkeley no Hume, and without Hume no Kant—and still less is it reasonable to ignore experience. At this point H. recurs to his favorite topic, speech, which as the expression of experience becomes the record of tradition. He is not impressed by Kant's effort to reduce speech to a shadowy existence like other "experiences." Speech is the object which reason can least afford to ignore, since it is reason itself in its sensible expression. Therefore speech of itself suffices to demolish the Kantian transcendentalism and the various forms of idealism which after it have been used for the construction of a world which is independent of the real world of tradition and experience.

I have not space to say more about the metacritique, and of most of the subsequent works I can make no mention at all. It is obvious that this pamphlet does not pretend to give a complete account of H. and his writings. I think of it as a challenge to some one abler than I and younger to write an adequate book.

But though this pamphlet cannot claim to be complete, it ought to be in some sense finished by a brief account of *Golgotha and Scheblimini*, which is commonly accounted the principal work of H., because it brings to a focus much that he said before. This was his penultimate production; but his last work, with which his pen fell from his hand, *A Flying Letter to Nobody the Notorious*, is in a sense included in *Golgotha*, since it was a reply to a strongly anti-Christian criticism of this book. By the time it was written both Lessing and Mendelssohn had died, and H. does honor to these two friends, one of them a recreant Jew and the other a Lutheran pastor of questionable faith, in the words of David's lament over Saul and Jonathan: "Lovely and pleasant in their lives, and in their death they were not divided. They were swifter than eagles, they were stronger than lions."

Quem semper acerbum
Semper honoratum (sic Di voluisti) habebo.

Golgotha and Scheblimini, "by a preacher in the wilderness," was published in 1784 as a reply to a book by Moses Mendelssohn called

Jerusalem, "or on religious authority and Judaism," which was published a year earlier. One may wonder that H. took the pains to answer this trivial book, which but for his attack upon it would soon have been forgotten. In part it was because Mendelssohn's superficial treatment of the themes, a dozen or more, which were the popular subjects of discussion in the age of Enlightenment was sure to be hailed with enthusiasm and needed to be rebuked. But chiefly it was because the observations disparaging to Christianity which were uttered by this liberal Jew could count upon hearty acclaim in Berlin where a liberal philosopher reigned in the palace of Sans Souci—although Judaism as well as Christianity was misrepresented in this book. Mendelssohn's book was divided into two parts, and so was H.'s reply. The second part, dealing with religion, is by far the more important.

As I have said, Mendelssohn dealt with themes which were much discussed in his day: the state of nature and the social contract, might and right, freedom and duty, liberty and despotism, state and church, temporal and eternal happiness, private property and the questionable advantage of benevolence.

H. began his attack by feigning to praise the book by quoting the eulogy with which Garve had recently introduced his translation of the first book of Cicero's *De officiis*: "It contains everything that can assure a book of a welcome reception and a hearty applause on the part of its readers, characteristics which all good books have always exhibited: perfect clarity in the individual thoughts and an easy and lucid connection in the development of them; obvious and useful truths in many passages, with indications of the noble and virtuous sentiments of the author." By this ironical eulogy Mendelssohn's slipshod book was damned at the start. I do not know if any other controversialist has ever used the same device for disposing of his opponent in advance of any direct criticism. H. then says, "But as for the theories of rights, duties and the social contract, I am not so well satisfied with the author's skill in resolving conflicts as common opinion and the judgment of his recent admirable translator and interpreter are with the treatise of old Cicero. About these controversial points and others like them I will entertain the thoughtful reader *kurz und gut* in the length and breadth and depth and height and crisscross and diagonally. But since there is a great gulf fixed between our religious and philosophical principles, fairness requires that I measure the author with himself and with no other, by the yardstick which he himself has provided." Thereupon H. proceeds to employ the precise words, phrases and sentences which Mendelssohn had used, but by putting them in a new connection he bestowed upon them a degree of precision and a significance which before they had conspicuously lacked. With infinite care he pieced them together, as in a mosaic picture which gives to the individual stones which compose it an importance which they did not have in themselves.

It was not an easy method to use, and no one who is not familiar with Mendelssohn's book could suspect that the author was answered out of his own mouth. Since that book cannot be quoted here except in part, I shall not linger long upon the section which deals with the secular topics I have enumerated above. But I would remark that perhaps no one in that age was better able than H. to rebuke the loose thinking which was characteristic of the Enlightenment. However, he did not pretend to answer conclusively the many questions which ought not to have been raised; it was enough to point out that the current discussions were rather about words than things. As an existentialist H. affirmed (using the words of Mendelssohn, the "theorist," who did not mean much by them) that "I am resolved to oppose constantly all theories and hypotheses, to speak only of facts, to wish to hear nothing but facts." He asserts that "a confusion of tongues which involves fundamental concepts does not remain without practical consequences." And, reverting to his favorite topic, he affirms that "the abuse of speech and the natural witness it bears is the grossest *perjury* and makes the transgressor of the first commandment of reason and its righteousness the worst enemy of man, a traitor and an adversary of the German uprightness upon which our worth and happiness depend." In this connection he takes Ezekiel's "valley of vision" (37:1) to mean "the valley of changing and confused concepts."

H. begins his attack by remarking that Mendelssohn, who takes many of his assumptions on faith, e.g. "the law of wisdom and goodness," "assumes and believes in a state of nature, which he contrasts with society, just as the dogmatists contrast it with a state of grace." He continues, "I do not begrudge him and the dogmatists this conviction, though for my part I am unable to form a clear conception of this hypothesis or to make any use of a notion which is so generally accepted by the *Buchstabmenschen* of our century [using the word Mendelssohn had treated as the equivalent of literati]. And I am no better off with respect to the social contract!" He adds as an *argumentum ad hominem*, "To both of us the divine and eternal covenant with Abraham and his seed must be far more important because of the blessing pronounced and promised to all nations of the earth on the ground of this solemn and documented contract."

"But with this I must leave the discussion of secular subjects in order to have room for the consideration of the far more important subject of religion, which is stressed by the title of Mendelssohn's book *Jerusalem* as well as by *Golgotha and Scheblimini*. Why Mendelssohn entitled his book by the name of a ruined city no critic has taken the pains to enquire, and perhaps the author himself does not know." For after its destruction by the Romans the old Jerusalem was completely abandoned, Hadrian's city of Ælia was not built on the same site, and the Christian city built by Constantine (which the good bishop Eusebius was fain to regard as the New Jerusalem foretold by the prophets) did not include the old sanctuaries, such as the site of the Temple, or even the Christian Church on Mount Sion; for it was built "outside the walls," where Christ suffered on Golgotha and where the empty tomb bore witness to the Resurrection.

Mendelssohn's philosophical Jerusalem has no relation to any city which ever was or is to be. "This adulterous philosophy is found on the meridian of Babalon." On the other hand, if Golgotha represents humiliation, Scheblimini meant to the author exaltation. As a good Lutheran he attached himself to "the name which Luther with Tisbitish or Socratic humor, gave to his *spiritum familiarum*, by which he meant the LORD who said unto David's Lord, 'Sit thou on my right hand!'" Mendelssohn's book, said H., should have been called Samaria, because this author, like the Samaritans who knew not what they worshipped, rejects the Prophets, and, having nothing left but the books of Moses, reduces religion to ritual law and "instructive ceremonial practices." H. repudiates rabbinical Judaism by quoting on the title page, in Mendelssohn's own translation, Jacob's blessing of Levi (Deut. 33:9-10), which assured to his tribe a monopoly of priestly ministrations. Below that he placed the words of Jeremiah 23:15: "Behold, I will feed them with wormwood and make them drink the water of gall: for from the prophets of Jerusalem is profaneness gone forth into all the land." About this motto he said in a letter, "The gall and the taste of wormwood came not from my wine press but from the wild grapes of *Jerusalem*, which were read with such general relish."

Mendelssohn's protest against the practice of requiring of clergymen an oath that they would hold and teach the doctrines prescribed by the Church was doubtless read with general relish in Berlin, especially by the liberal clergymen who were Mendelssohn's friends; but these same clergymen would be bitterly offended by his *obiter dictum* that it is highly derogatory to the dignity of ministers of religion to receive pecuniary rewards. This observation, of course, was meant to give offense. In form, but not in spirit, it was the objection the early Quakers made against "a hireling ministry." H. did not have to make a serious reply to this policy of pin pricks; for the whole thing was put in a ludicrous light when Mendelssohn explained that in rabbinical Judaism the minister of circumcision received no fee as a reward for his skill in handling the knife, but was content with the honor of presiding at the banquet which followed this ceremony.

Alluding to the vain effort of the good Lavater to induce him to be baptized (just as the good Jacobi tried in vain to convert Lessing), Mendelssohn said, "But, my dear man, if it is true that the cornerstone of my house threatens to fall, is it reasonable for me to save my possessions by removing them to the upper floors? Am I more secure there? Christianity, as you know, is built upon Judaism, and when that falls Christianity must collapse with it."

"Never," he said, "have I openly attacked the Christian religion, and never will I enter into conflict with its genuine adherents. But, lest I be reproached again on this score, I would say in this connection that I had in my hands more victorious weapons against Christianity, if I were disposed to use them. Here, at all events, I have adduced nothing new against the Christians, nothing which has not been said and repeated countless times by Jews and naturalistic philosophers, and been answered again and again by their opponents."

Nevertheless, Mendelssohn was well aware that he had something new to say, something which he believed would prove surprising to his Jewish as well as to his Christian readers, and perhaps would seem equally "hard" to both.

"It is true," he says, "that I recognize no other eternal truths but those which by human power are not only rendered comprehensible but can be demonstrated and maintained. I regard this as an essential feature of the Jewish religion, and I believe that this teaching constitutes a characteristic difference between Judaism and the Christian religion. To put it briefly, I believe that Judaism knows nothing of a revealed religion in the sense that this is conceived by the Christians. The Israelites had a divine law but no dogmas, no 'saving truths,' no universal rational propositions. Those propositions are called eternal truths which are not subject to time but remain the same in eternity. Apart from these eternal truths there are also temporal, historical truths, things which occur at one moment of time and perhaps are never repeated. Of this sort are all the truths of history in the widest sense. The necessary truths are grounded upon reason. On the other hand, the authority of the narrator and his credibility contribute the only evidence in historical matters. Without authority the truth of history disappears with the event. Among all the commandments of the law there is not a single one which reads, 'Thou shalt believe.' For faith was not commanded. In fact, the original word which commonly is translated by Faith properly means in most places [in the O.T.] confident reliance upon a pledge or promise. When it is a question of the truths of reason we do not speak of believing but of recognizing and knowing. Historical truths, according to their nature can be received only by faith. It is authority alone which gives them the requisite evidence; and these reports were confirmed to the Nation by miracles and were supported by an authority sufficient to raise them above doubt and scruple."

This long quotation must be made in order to understand H.'s reply. But also because it contains truths which need to be heard today, and which never so much needed to be heard as in the age of Enlightenment, when all theologians, whether they were rationalists or dogmatists, agreed in supposing that faith meant assent to abstract rational propositions which are believed to be the expression of universal and eternal truths.

Perhaps in that generation no one would be so little surprised or disconcerted by these hard sayings as was H. He recognized that there was truth in the passage I have quoted, but he convicted Mendelssohn of misrepresenting both Judaism and Christianity. He said, "I entirely agree with Hr. Mendelssohn that Judaism knows nothing of a *revealed* religion in the sense he gives to this word. That is to say, nothing was made known to the Jews and entrusted to them by God except the sensible vehicle of the *mysteries*, the *shadow of good things to come,* not the substance of those things, the actual transmission of which God had reserved to a Mediator, High Priest, Prophet and King, higher than Moses, Aaron, David and Solomon. The characteristic difference between Judaism and Christianity has nothing to do with mediate or immediate *revelation* in the sense in which this word is used by Jews and naturalistic philosophers, nothing to do with *eternal truths* and *dogmas*, nor with ceremonial or moral law, but has to do only with temporal historical truths which occurred at one moment of time and never will be repeated. The characteristic difference between Christianity and Judaism has to do with *historical truths* not only of past but of future time, which were foretold and prophesied, and which according to their nature cannot be received except by *faith*. Jewish authority alone avails to give them requisite evidence; and also these memorabilia of past and future time were confirmed by miracles, by the trustworthiness of the witnesses and the tradition, and by the evidence of actual fulfillment, which suffices to raise faith above all Talmudic and dialectical doubts and scruples."

I have given here only a sample, a mere taste, of H.'s polemic, and there is no space for many more items. But I would call attention to his reproof of Mendelssohn for defining the Church as "a public institution for the education of men with respect to their relationship to God"—after Mendelssohn himself had affirmed "the infinite disproportion (or disrelationship) between man and God." In view of this disrelationship it is clear that the primary function of the Church is to re-establish the relationship which has been broken.

It was characteristic of Mendelssohn to affirm that "in the strictest sense it is not in accord with the truth nor compatible with the best interests of men to separate so sharply temporal and eternal interests. Man will not have an everlasting share in the eternal: his eternity is only an endless temporality. The concepts are confused when one contrasts temporal welfare with eternal happiness." Here he preaches what even Haeckel stigmatized as "the bad eternity." H., as a thoroughgoing eschatologist, insists upon eternity in the good sense. "This adulterous philosophy," he says, "speaks half in the language of Ashdon (Nehem. 13:24) and not in the pure Jewish idiom." He expresses himself in the pure Jewish idiom when he says, "The *revealed* religion of Christianity is rightly called *faith*, trust, confidence, the cheerful childlike assurance based upon the divine promises and the glorious fulfillment of life from one clarity to another, until it attains the complete revelation and apocalypse which transforms that which was at first the hidden mystery, only apprehended by *faith*, into fullness of vision, face to face."

In the serious conclusion to this book H. handed to Mendelssohn hard nuts to crack when he affirmed that "skepticism of the truth and the credulity of self-deceit are (to use this author's own words) symptoms as inseparable as the alternation of chills and heat in fever"; and he said that "all human knowledge is 'in part,' and all human arguments founded upon reason consist either of *faith in the truth* and *doubt of untruth*—or of *faith in untruth* and *doubt* of the truth." About the "bad eternity" he says only this in conclusion: "Thoughtful reader, *what concern to us is the peace which this world gives?* We know for certain that the Day of the LORD will come as a thief in the night, when they will say, Peace, peace, but there is no peace, then will destruction soon overtake them—but may HE the God of peace, who is higher than all reason, sanctify us totally, that our spirit along with our soul and body may be kept blameless unto the *future*. He that bareth witness says, Yea, I come quickly! Amen!"

www.ingramcontent.com/pod-product-compliance
Lightning Source LLC
Chambersburg PA
CBHW061517040426
42450CB00008B/1662